DOGS WHO SMILE

THOMAS DUNNE BOOKS
St. Martin's Griffin
New York

THOMAS DUNNE BOOKS.
An imprint of St. Martin's Press.

www.thomasdunnebooks.com
www.stmartins.com

Library of Congress Cataloging-in-Publication Data Available Upon Request

ISBN 978-1-250-03308-6 (paper over board)
ISBN 978-1-250-03323-9 (e-book)

First published in Great Britain by Ebury Press, an imprint of Ebury Publishing,
a Random House Company

First U.S. Edition: July 2013

10 9 8 7 6 5 4 3 2 1

The Random House Group Limited supports The Forest Stewardship Council®(FSC®), the leading
international forest certification organisation. Our books carrying the FSC label are printed on
FSC® certified paper. FSC is the only forest certification scheme endorsed by the leading
environmental organisations, including Greenpeace. Our paper procurement policy can be found at
www.randomhouse.co.uk/environment

Printed and bound in China by Toppan Leefung

FOR TALLY

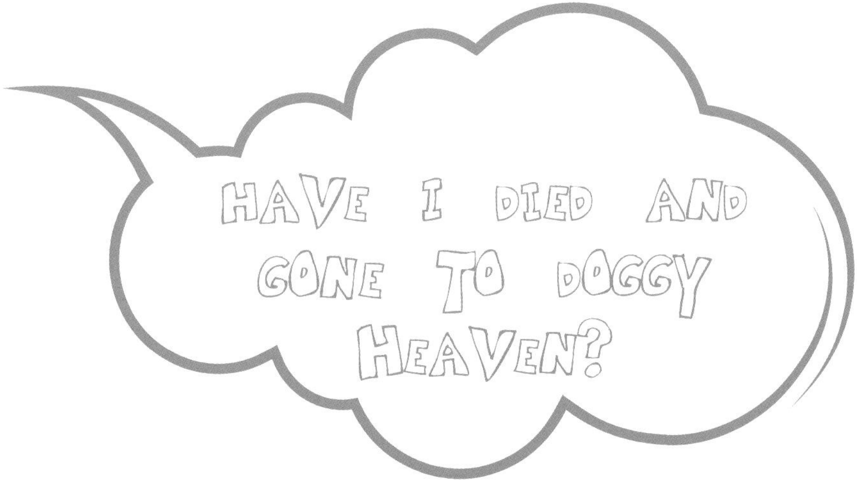
HAVE I DIED AND GONE TO DOGGY HEAVEN?

IF I SAY 'CHEESE'
ANY LONGER I M
GONNA START
DROOLING...

"And don't even think about blaming that one on me..."

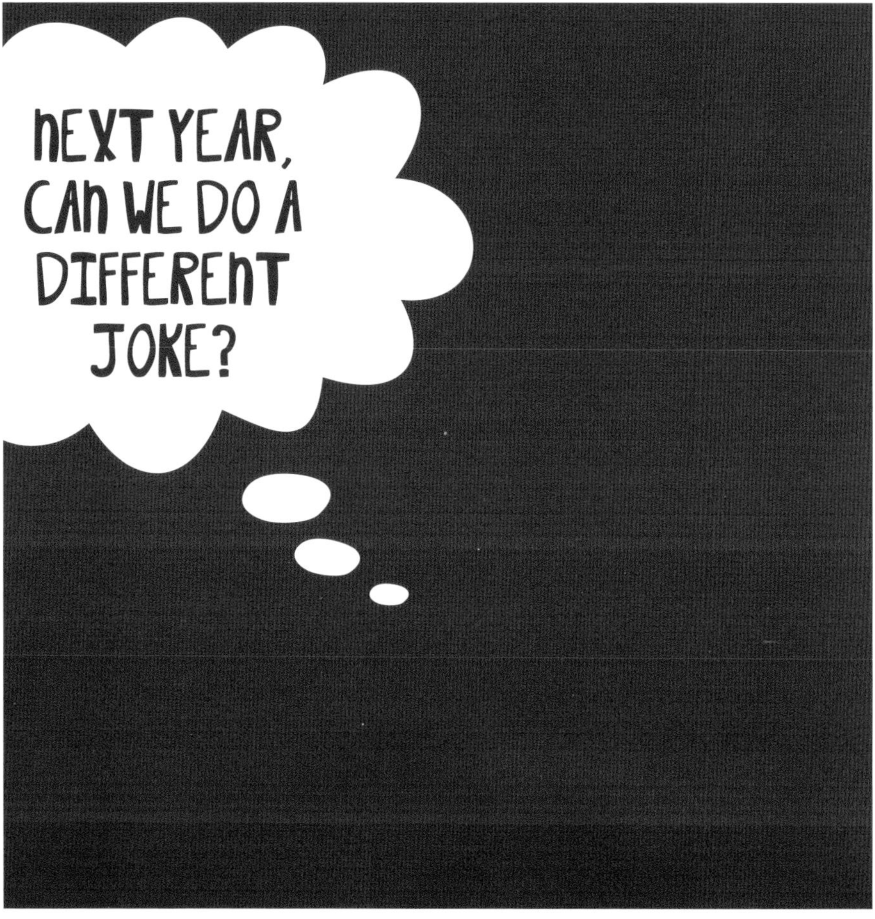
NEXT YEAR, CAN WE DO A DIFFERENT JOKE?

"Quick! Dude!
YouTube this!"

"OK, SO FIRST WE HIT THE CLEAN SHEETS, THEN ROLL ON THE WHITE CARPET..."

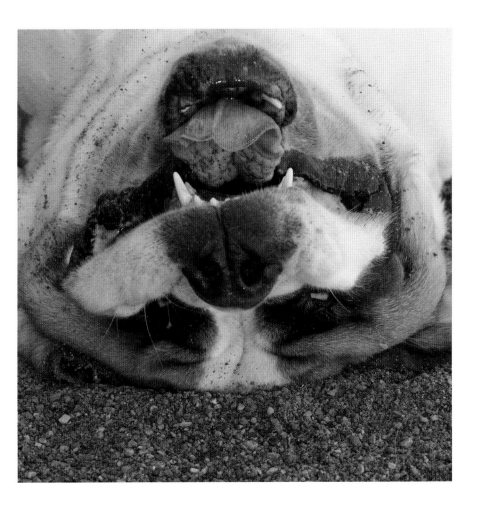

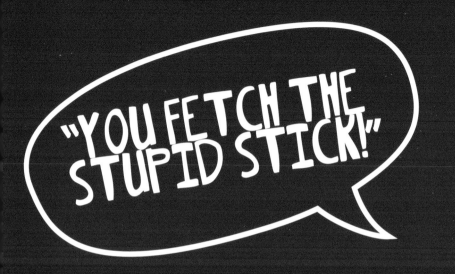

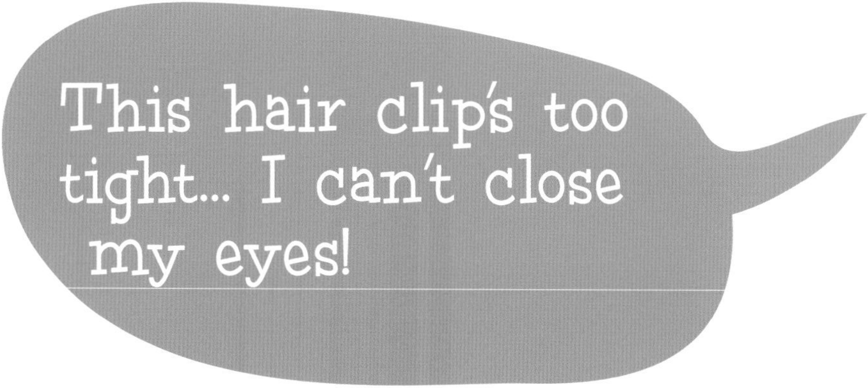
This hair clip's too tight... I can't close my eyes!

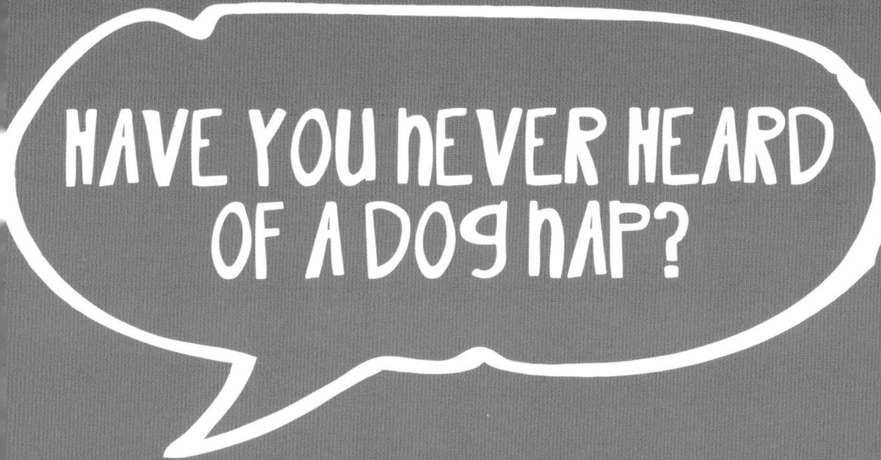
HAVE YOU NEVER HEARD OF A DOG NAP?

"You sit and throw, I run and fetch. It's a win-win situation!"

"ALL TOGETHER NOW... DOGGY PADDLE!"

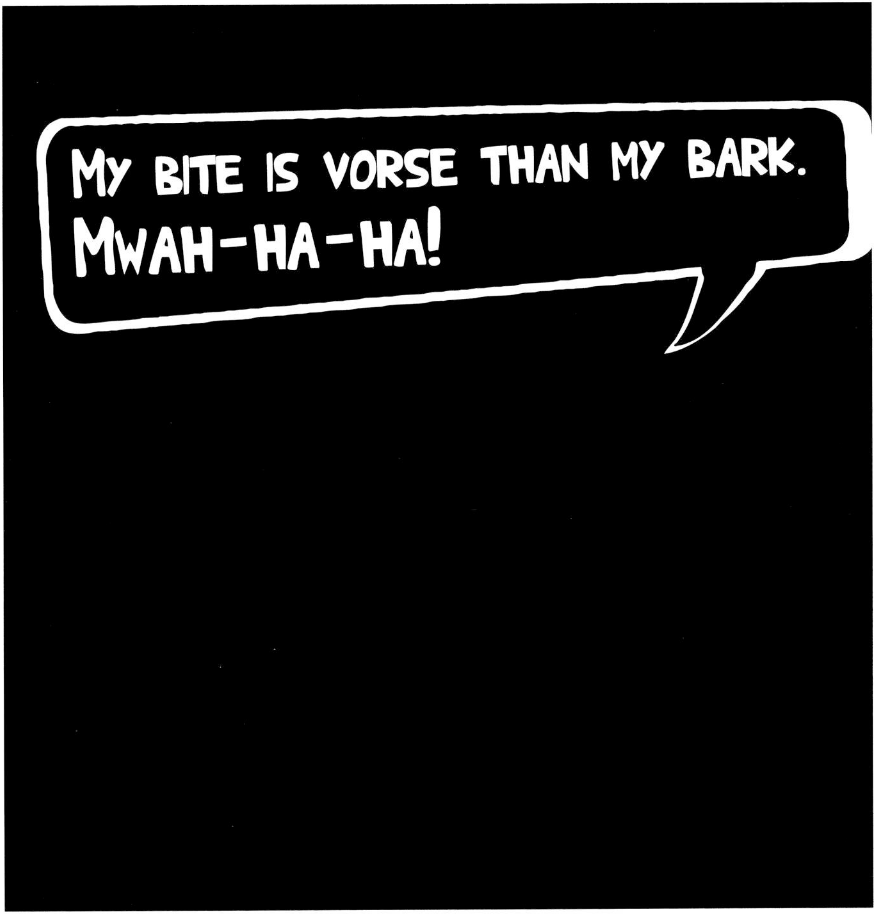
MY BITE IS VORSE THAN MY BARK. MWAH-HA-HA!

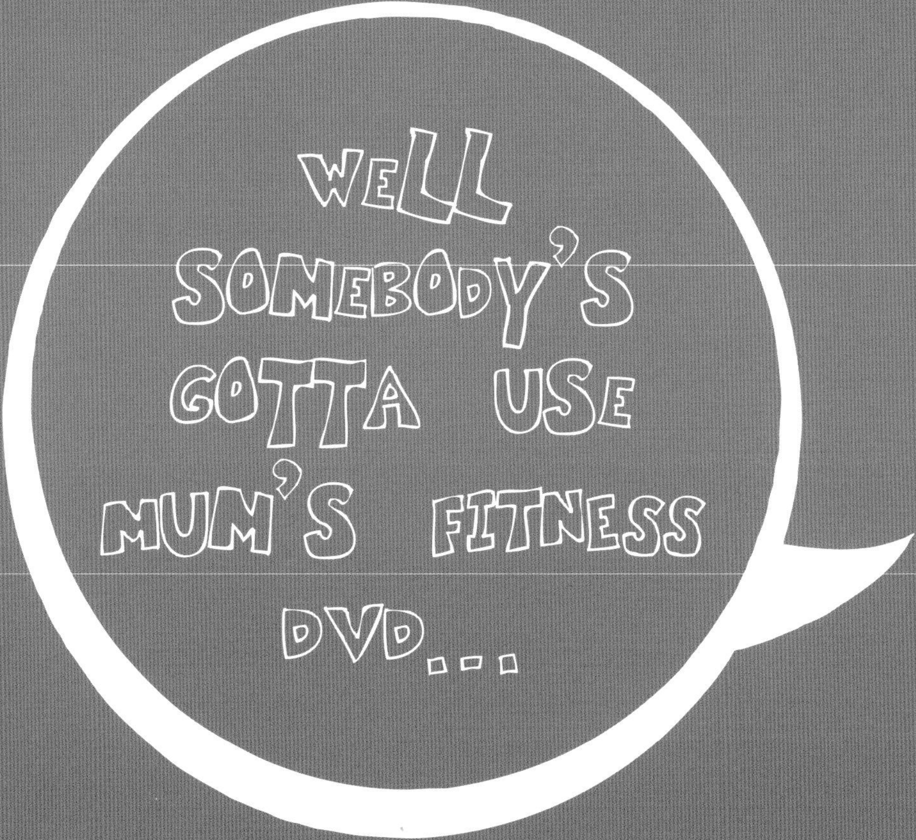
WELL SOMEBODY'S GOTTA USE MUM'S FITNESS DVD...

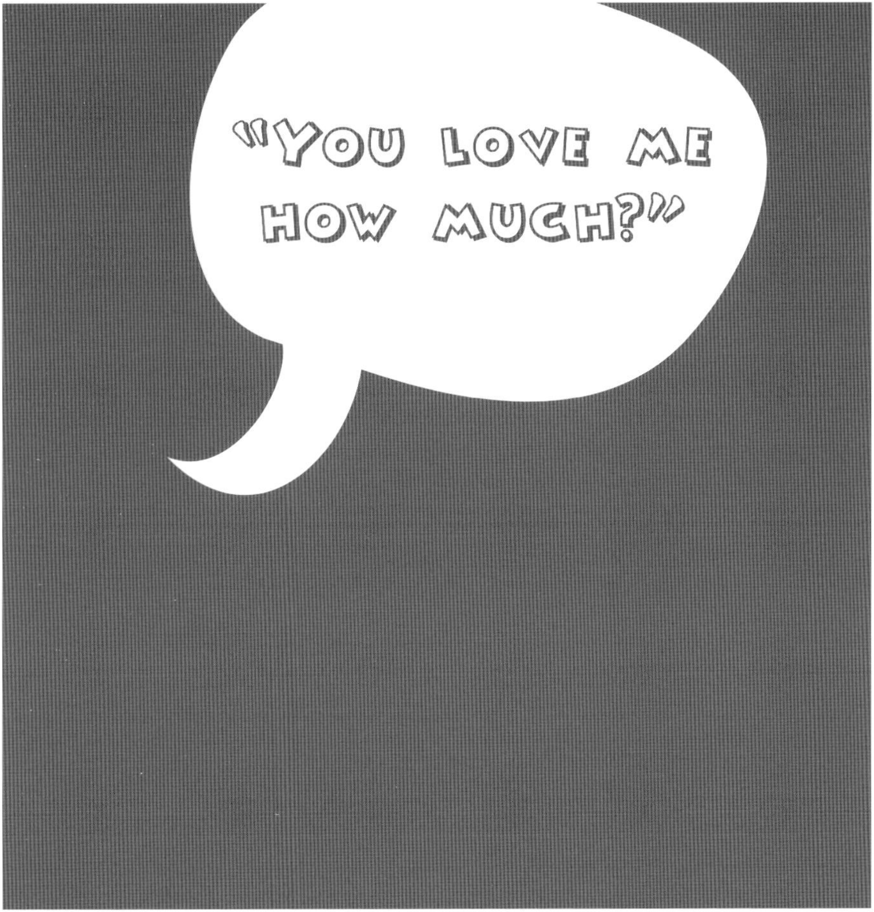
"YOU LOVE ME HOW MUCH?"

"IF I SQUINT, THE POSTMAN WILL THINK I'M SLEEPING, AND THEN... BANG!"

HI, MY NAME IS MAX. AND MY SPECIALIST SUBJECT IS LAMPPOSTS OF THE WORLD

"See this arrow? Apply biscuits now!"

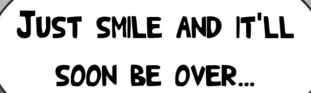

"MAYBE THE WIND MACHINE WAS A BAD IDEA?"

"BE HONEST, DOES THIS COLLAR MAKE MY EARS LOOK BIG?"

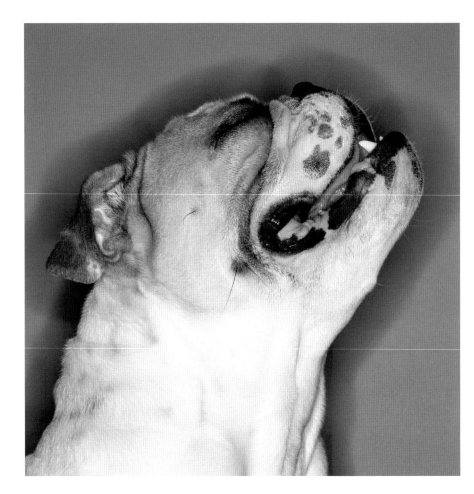

"UP A BIT,
LEFT A
BIT... THAT'S
NIIIIICE!"

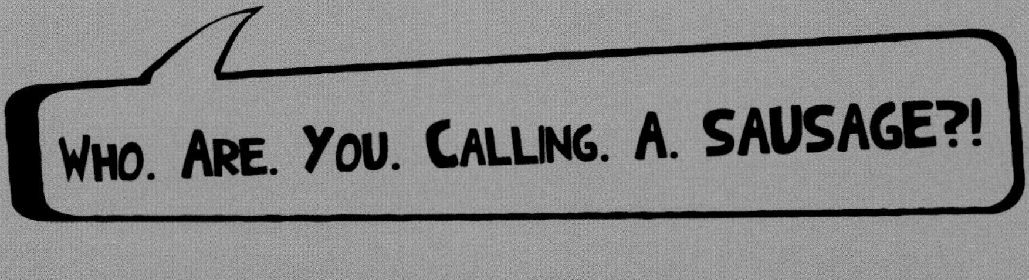
WHO. ARE. YOU. CALLING. A. SAUSAGE?!

I know she's starting to look like me... It kinda creeps me out...

Picture Credits